A DIFFERENT
Point of View

A DIFFERENT
Point of View

GREGORY HIGHTOWER

Dedicated to Junko Hightower
A tigress no matter what. . .

"You'll meet people from different walks of life
but still on common ground" – Gregory Hightower

Contents

Chapter 1

The Value

There's a lot of significance placed upon a child's birth
It seems we tend to forget or overlook that person's worth
Everyone was brought to the Earth as seeds that were planted
Some of us are incapable of that which gets taken for granted

People don't last forever, the clock started as soon as we entered the womb
And you should assume anyone's life at any moment can end up in a tomb
The most recent words and encounter with a person may be the very last
You can't change the past or place a broken heart into a plaster cast

Imagine the person you love just disappears tomorrow
You'll feel hollow and look for a good place to wallow
Human relations isn't my profession so this is entirely at your discretion
My suggestion is that you view everyone as your most prized possession

You can't put a price on a human being because we're priceless
But you can set them on a pedestal and call them your highness
You don't have to be an expert to cherish, it's okay to be a novice
Every moment matters because death will surely fulfill its promise

This should be carried out every day from sunrise to sunset like Ramadan
The task is simple and not exhausting compared to running a marathon
When you drive down memory lane I hope you avoid an awful avenue
Remember to value others in the same way you want them to value you

This World

This world is orchestrated for me to lose
It focuses on bad rather than good news
It has helped me see things with more than just my eyes
And over time made human nature not come as a surprise

This world tries to program you to follow a specific route
Like a parent raising their child, you know what I'm talking about
They want you to do this and that or get beat like its boxing bout
Don't pout because they brought you in this world and can take you out

This world likes to give idiots a chance at power, profit and protest
You know guys like George Bush, Donald Trump and Kanye West
It has a month that is specifically dedicated to African American history
Interesting, because that's American history but I won't let that get to me

This world likes to punish you if you're different in any kind of way
Things that you can't change like if you happen to be gay
It doesn't want you to think or ask any questions
Just accept the indoctrination and all of its suggestions

This world relies on immigration since we're divided by nation
But enjoys coming together in a crisis for a war invasion
It has invested in weaponry and made war its number one specialty
And let the actions of a few people cause you to question a refugee

This world is hostile and could possibly self-destruct
Possibly from global warming or people who want it to combust
You can't even get on plane with lotion because security will try to take it
They tell you to take off your shoes, take off your belt and then get naked

It's safe to say things are out of control like cops in the USA
But we can still make a change like a GPS and find a way
This world can do anything; it made smart phones with auto correct
Instagram and Facebook so we can stalk each other on the internet

This world is imperfect so that means we need improvements
Just like the grades of people who aren't proactive students
I hope this doesn't sound like a rant; I just want the madness to stop
Help me change this world, pretty please, with a cherry on top

Attachment

You're in love to death and your actions show the depth
Willing to give anything for love even your last breath
Beautiful at first like summer and now you have to suffer
Because you discovered your significant other has another

It feels horrendous, you feel like you're going to lose your mind
This man has crossed the line like an area that's excessively mined
You can either leave, try to make reparations or get even
The outcome will definitely be as ugly as sin inside a demon

You can't just leave because time is involved
Memories and years, so this can be resolved
I presume it can be fixed but he has a severe condition
Pretty faces weaken him so maybe that's an addiction

Getting even could work if you want to use men to make amends
Your options are endless like his relatives or one of his best friends
This can play out in any way regardless if it's tomorrow or today
I can even give you a mental display, he'll be begging for you to stay

He knows exactly what to do and say in order for you to be okay
Maybe things will reset and he'll change or maybe he'll go astray
You can forgive and show compassion but this was no accident
Understandable though, people can't easily detach like an attachment

Forgiveness is moving on after being stabbed in the back or gutted from the front
Forgiveness isn't completely forgetting what occurred during that heinous stunt
Forgiveness will, nine out of ten, be you excusing people who aren't sorry
Forgiveness is trying to bury the hatchet in a trench the size of a quarry

Forgiveness is usually one-sided so expect to never receive an apology
Forgiveness doesn't exist in everyone and that's just human biology
Forgiveness means overcoming the pain not rekindling the old flame
Forgiveness will be taken for granted because you're sweet like aspartame

Forgiveness requires a long period of time and there's no set deadline
Forgiveness helps you with the hate bottled up that doesn't age like wine
Forgiveness doesn't mean that the pain will eventually fade away
Forgiveness makes you stronger and I know that sounds cliché

Forgiveness has no price which means your money is worthless
Forgiveness would always be sold out if it was available for purchase
Forgiveness can calm the fight you're having within and comfort your heart
Forgiveness shows you that nonviolence can also be used as a martial art

Forgiveness will eventually make sense and open your eyes like an eyelid
Forgiveness is your best bet so don't wait too long to place your bid
Forgiveness beats revenge and going to prison for first-degree murders
Forgiveness allows you to rebuild so make sure you use new girders

Family is always and forever and that's just our fate
I guess misbehaving correlates with DNA so it's innate
That's why they can't help but attempt to seduce my spouse
Even steal from dying relatives while they're still in the house

Family says negative things to each other on a regular basis
Enjoys alcoholic beverages then violence, goodness gracious
Shoot verbal bullets until one hits a sensitive spot
I think our family bloodline is just about ready to clot

Family enjoys creating rumors about you and going on a gossip
spree
Now I'm the villain for wanting to take a chainsaw to the family tree
I wonder if our lineage expressed their love in this way as well
We must be related to a warlock because we're as cursed as a
witch's spell

Family in my eyes are oftentimes considered strangers
They let me couch surf and provide shelter like a hangar
Strangers could also be regarded as your family
Begging for money constantly without any vanity

Family can't possibly be permanent since that belief is based
off of love
Just like the stabs in the back and they don't even try to hide
the glove
I guess that's the way it goes since blood is thicker than a water hose
I'm just not entirely sure if my beloved kindred are my family or foes

Don't Be

Don't be a parent that is insensitive and doesn't care how their child is feeling
The type that says and does whatever they want when their temper hits the ceiling
Don't be a child because that means the house has no adult supervision
Children see and hear everything so be mindful of every decision

Don't believe words aren't so harmful because that isn't true
Children carry that into adulthood in what they say and do
Don't believe everyone is keeping your child out of harm's way
Regular company can always make things appear to be okay

Don't be a parent who is ignorant to the long term effects of neglect
One day your child could struggle with intimacy and trying to connect
Don't be an alcoholic on top of being physically abusive
Maybe the child inherits that or their life becomes reclusive

Don't believe abuse isn't deeply rooted and passed down by generation
Otherwise things could eventually lead to a childcare investigation
Don't believe staying in a violent home is better than a broken home
At least one is finished and you can protect your child like chrome
Don't be surprised how your child behaves when they become older
They might not want you around and then show you a cold shoulder
Don't be a bad role model and certainly not their adversary
Be everything in a friend and not the type that's imaginary

American

So proud to be an American and I completely understand
But we're not the only home of the brave and free land
We don't have to categorize everything by ethnicity
I'm referring to African and Latin American specifically

America is a great country but we aren't the greatest
Instead of being pro-war we should be anti-racist
Our problems are unfortunate but they aren't the most tragic
There are places where avoiding explosives is a daily tactic

Foreigners know a whole lot about us and that should be mutual
We could visit some countries because a lot of them are beautiful
It's okay to be a bit patriotic but let's get away from being idiotic
Focus on education and not YouTube videos that become iconic

We're not the standard for the entire world so don't be so self-centered
Our nation is very young and that's something that should be remembered
Don't believe everything in the media, not every terrorist is a Muslim
Violence and insults towards a specific group shouldn't be a custom

The majority of us are lazy, obese and probably because of the food industry
Between them, the government and an enemy there's a whole lot of symmetry
Aside from all of that I would say we're pretty good Samaritans
We should be great world citizens and not ugly Americans

Chapter 2

Change

We demand and expect so much from the people we love the most
Love is still there even when we use each other as a whipping post
No matter what happens or any problem that occurs, it's always fixable
It's understandable, I suppose, since love is supposedly unconditional

Some things we can't foresee like when a person undergoes metamorphosis
Then love begins a similar process and changes form like a contortionist
Now the person you used to know has evolved into someone unfamiliar
But we're supposed to change; no one in life should remain a caterpillar

Maybe it was the people around them, traumatic events or change in objectives
Whatever it was it has created a rift and exposed two different perspectives
Maybe it was your fault and they finally noticed you're this vile individual
They don't want you around or even a thought of you to be residual

Don't be upset that old person is gone; it's not for the worse or the worst
Whether good or bad we all made a change but one of us did it first
As you look back through the years, things will become contact lens clear
Change is inevitable like a cashier and life will always make paths veer

You realize that people come and they go in and out of our lives
There simply isn't enough space for all of them, we're not hard
drives
Whoever they have become you should feel happiness and not
contempt
Remember change is an acronym, can happen anytime nobody
gets exempt

Religion

Human programming is an interesting thing if you know what I mean
I can get a human being to join the team if I have a good scheme...
You can assist me by being unguided and weak minded
Don't worry about the rules; you'll frequently be reminded...

This is a great life decision so follow me and pay attention
The law of the land is my conviction so it's time for your submission...
I don't want to be in control I just want to save your soul
It's okay if it separates us from other people as a whole...

Although you've done nothing wrong you must ask for forgiveness
Never seek vengeance or harm any person but I accept penance...
These are the only stipulations that will keep you from damnation
I'm not Satan or asking you to sacrifice a child for expiation...

If you're suffering from anything come pray and make a confession
Anything at all like worldly music, sexual desires or being a lesbian...
Don't be so skeptical it's good to live your life based off of a book
Don't be concerned with your cash donations, God isn't a crook...

Love your neighbor but avoid him or her if they're a nonbeliever
It's all your choice but that's not how you should spend your leisure...
God loves each and every one of his children and never hates
Just don't behave like Lucifer and you'll be safe in the pearly gates...

Love

Love is many things but it's the greatest emotion
It doesn't really ask for much except your devotion
If you try looking for it you'll just waste your time
I'm not playing with your mind but love is blind

Love should be instilled in every little boy and girl
Things would be more clear like a diamond or pearl
Love is permanent, always and forever
No matter what, it'll bring us together

Love is a challenge and for some it's impossible
It has a great fall and there's always an obstacle
Love should be expressed but some prefer abuse
It has a long journey so make sure you tie your shoes

Love conquers all and reigns supreme
It can put a stop to hate's evil scheme
Love can satisfy each and every single person
It'll bring happiness but it'll always leaves a burden

Love is taking a chance and that could be dangerous
Sometimes it's pleasant and sometimes it's heinous
Be prudent with love because it involves more than you
And if you say, "I Love You", make sure that it's true

Accompanied By Anger

Amazing how swift your emotions can get the best of you
Then you lose your mind and there's no search and rescue
One incident becomes a lot of pain and stress
And anger overcomes you with complete success

You don't think wisely or choose any nice words to blurt
Only scanning for something that will tremendously hurt
You'll eventually reach your goal and here's what will happen
Horrible satisfaction manipulated by anger in a way you didn't
imagine

It will decimate your friendship or your relationship
Good luck coming back from this like a vacation trip
It's easy to release words since we have loose lips
But you can't withdraw them back like a waiter's tips

Anger lights a match, creates a hot head and that's a burning
platform
Adrenaline fuels that fire until you calm down and become
lukewarm
Similar to spontaneous combustion and you're headed for
self-destruction
Your temporary mental dysfunction will cause you to suffer a
repercussion

The aftermath will be an awkward and uncomfortable atmosphere
Get ahold of your anger before it destroys everything like a
bombardier
This isn't aiding your health so it would be wise to transcend
If it's hard to comprehend then try being on the receiving end

I Hate

I hate you with all of my heart and it will only get worse
There's no saving me, so no need for a doctor or a nurse
I hate that I hate you because that just means you're on my mind
I want you to listen to a recording of me saying everything unkind

I hate that you are given an equal chance at happiness just like me
If only I could halt that and make you suffer to a far degree
I hate that I'm coming off as someone who's bitter
I just can't help it because you're equivalent to Hitler

I hate that you have loved ones that give you love and affection
I hope they get ill and you watch them slowly die from an infection
I hate that I can't give you all of this hate that I'm harboring inside
I'll settle for a kick up your backside then watching you drink cyanide

I hate your parents more than I hate you and you can imagine why
I hope you go blind on one side and someone carves out the other eye
I hate you more than I hate the Internal Revenue Service
I want to watch you crawl naked across a volcanic surface

I hate that I can't cure this hatred by drinking water and taking medicine
I hope you end up in a weird experiment and turn into a mutated specimen
I hate complete strangers who do things that remind me of you
I hope you get diagnosed with Alzheimer's and never have a clue

I hate that I've given you my time and all of this recognition
I want to use you for target practice with unlimited ammunition
I hate that I give you power over me and it's not even my fault
I wish you were the one wounded and I was holding the salt

One-Sided

Your heart's in the right place but it's completely alone
Giving all this love but not a trace of theirs is shown
It's great to accept others for who they are
But only when they're decent and up to par

You're simply getting gypped out of your time
And they'll never care or say a word like a mime
You may not see it just like a solar eclipse
They're benefitting off of you like scholarships

You're giving eighty while receiving twenty; I wonder what you're buying
There's no denying that a friendship should be equal along with satisfying
You have love to give and I know there's quite a lot
They may seem heartless but their heart just has a clot

Of course it's hard to swallow so you can treat it like bubblegum
Looking out for number one should always be the rule of thumb
Don't allow yourself to be secondary when they're your priority
Unless you want to settle for less but that's strange like a deformity

Sometimes you can't listen to your heart so you listen to your gut
Severing all ties might make you feel like a new person and uncut
Driving down a dead end road has never gotten anyone anywhere
You might as well be a beggar expecting to become a billionaire

A true friendship will feel genuine and it won't be tentative
You won't feel sick to your stomach like you need a lenitive
You have only been misdirected so don't think you're misguided
There may be many angles but sometimes things are just one-sided

Life

Life is short but it's long enough for you to enjoy
It will always surprise you with some insane ploy
Life is black and white with a whole lot of grey
It's never simple, always a catch like a bouquet

Life occasionally kicks you down in hopes of kicking you even lower
It doesn't want you to flourish so good luck avoiding this lawnmower
Life is so spontaneous that at this very moment something is coming
The strong survive it but even for them things become mind-numbing

Life is hard but don't worry because it won't last forever
Assume there will always be resistance for any endeavor
Life is a lesson everyday with more than a mid-term and a final exam
Hopefully you'll learn but it'll take some time just like a traffic jam

Life isn't a female dog because dogs are very delightful
It might be a person though, people are often spiteful
Life starts off as a rat race then turns into a stampede
It requires insurance because nothing is guaranteed

Life is a set up and it's usually betting against you so consider it opposition
A fight that'll put you in critical condition and then straight to the mortician
Life will vex you because it always brings you face to face with adversity
If you want to expect the unexpected then you can expect a perversity

If you allow it to do so then life will pass you by
Never live it in regret because the end is nigh
Life will position you to live a certain lifestyle
It isn't pretty at all but you should still smile

Chapter 3

I Was Taught

I was taught to be a good boy and listen to my elders
If I didn't then eventually sparks would fly like welders
Say please, thank you and excuse me so you leave a good impression
Stay in school if you care about your life and want a good profession

I was taught to never disrespect your parents if they were always around
You'll meet people from different walks of life but still on common ground
Always be on time because if you're late then someone will notice
Hard work pays off so never call in sick unless it's a fatal prognosis

I was taught to refrain from using foul language, don't cuss like a sailor
Take the utmost pride in your appearance; it wouldn't hurt to see a tailor
If you can't take care of yourself then you can't take care of anyone
Kindness gets taken for weakness so don't be so sweet like a honeybun

I was taught that a man has to be strong and never ever cry
Yawning should be the only thing that puts a tear in your eye
Always have a plan but also expect to get hit
Things always get harder but you don't get to quit

I was taught your word is your bond, so be a man of your word
Only believe half of what you see and absolutely nothing you heard
Some experiences will leave a bad taste in your mouth but don't be so bitter
If you want to attain anything out of life then you have to be a go-getter

I was taught there will always be you in the center of trouble
Never allow things to go to your head so always be humble
People are going to talk about you behind your back
Failure is acceptable but always gets back on track

A Better Man

Always room for improvement or so they say
Be a better man just like there's a better way
He'll never be perfect but he will always try to get rid of any inadequacy
Always proud and stand up for what he believes in like giving advocacy

He's no better than you are and even if he was, he would only be modest Awful thoughts at times, to be honest, but his mind is one of the broadest
He has a tremendous heart but it beats quietly
Loves his privacy and not a big fan of society

He would give you his first and his last dollar
He often tries to be wise but he's not a scholar
Words can't describe how much he's been through, not even in cursive
A sweet hearted kind of guy but knows when it's time to be assertive

He would prefer to be your friend rather than your adversary
Peaceful like a monastery but can easily turn into a mercenary
Never does harm to anyone but doesn't always get the same treatment
Difficult to figure out but easy to understand like a spoken agreement

He's in a constant war with fighting his demons and female temptations
That's a bad combination but those aren't even the worse revelations
He will always make an effort to reason but he's known for getting even
Hates to be a part of the bandwagon so he's content with being a heathen

Enjoys the people who mean the world to him
But he can easily live without all of them
Sometimes he gets sidetracked but he's sticking to his game plan
Doing the best he can but it'll be awhile until he's a better man

My Brother

I never really cared for what was on the outside, only the internal
We aren't related at all but I still get this feeling that we're fraternal
The skin color, the culture and the home of record never mattered
Only respect, loyalty, love and a friendship that's not easily tattered

We mesh so well, always see eye to eye and never act violently
Thank you for not taking me through the stages of sibling rivalry
I have no need to complain because everything is simple and plain
Unlike Cain and Abel, we're able to support each other like a cane

I wish we lived closer but the distance makes the heart grow fonder
Always cherish the brotherly love and never allow it to squander
We can't be brothers from another mother but we can be kindred spirits
One day we can take all of our pictures and open up best friend exhibits

I can always rely on you because you're by my side at all times like pinstripes
I would give my life for you, but that's only if we have different blood types
You're a true friend indeed and I want the both of us to succeed
May our roots always run deep like trouble or a garden weed

Thank you for being more than what I could ever ask for
For evermore a life saver in high water until I can get ashore
You'll always have a place in my home and someone to vouch
Just don't turn into a grouch if I make you sleep on the couch

A Good Woman

She's hard to find so I would call her a four leaf clover
Always willing to fight for you like a hostile takeover
She will always be by your side, she has unbelievable endurance
All she wants in return is your love and occasional reassurance

She watches over you when you're fast asleep
Her value is priceless so forget about being cheap
She will respect you for as long as you respect her
She can be as hard as titanium or as soft as fur

She is one of a kind which means she is one out of five
The type of woman that makes you happy to be alive
You're always on her mind and never have to question if she's
loyal
If you do anything that will cause her to leave, you won't like the
recoil

She remembers everything you say so be mindful of your tongue
The only thing that will takes precedence over you, are her young
She doesn't need eyes to see because she has her intuition
Better than any detective looking for proof to a supposition

She can't replace your mother but she could give her a run for
her money
She will comfort you when your nights are terrible and days aren't
sunny
Being with her is just like winning the lottery
But don't give up the lottery for debauchery

It makes her happy to put a smile on your face
Always return the favor by showing her grace
She can look at many things and tell if they are a bad omen
If she's treating you better than herself then she's a good woman

Something Different

I was born this way and that shouldn't be an issue
People are very cold though, colder than an igloo
I'm viewed as a lesser person as if I were a cannibal
The frowns, whispers and hatred are almost tangible

I'm not allowed to be gay because that's a bad direction to swing
Whatever I do is disgusting but straight couples do the same thing
I thought gay rights and civil rights were interchangeable
And if they aren't then it should be easily explainable

There is nothing wrong with me but I'm supposedly a degenerate
Wherever people have learned this I hope the source is legitimate
Sometimes I feel completely alone, helpless and defenseless
So much judgment over something that is only my business

I'm supposed to feel ashamed because what I am and what I do is immoral
I'll avoid discussing that topic since it will probably be an endless quarrel
I wouldn't be any other way and plus it helps me to see who has a closed mind
In addition to a weak mind that will believe anything if they're led by the blind

I'm just a man who has preferences other than yours
No need to wish me dead and gone like dinosaurs
I've done nothing wrong but the majority will never see me as their equivalent
I don't understand why I can't be different without people acting belligerent

Be Happy

No one will ever love you as much as you do
Happiness should be like a statue with a tattoo
Permanent and everything to maintain it should be pertinent
If it's not then you might be trapped in encirclement

Follow your heart because it deserves what it wants
Don't become daunted and succumb to people's taunts
It's healthy for you so go ahead and take a chance
You love it for a reason and that isn't happenstance

You don't have to listen to anyone or live up to their expectations
There are no limitations, only people's negative exclamations
Make it an undertaking and don't allow it to end up with an
undertaker
I'm not a matchmaker but missing out on what you love is a
heartbreaker

Pleasure awaits you if you can overcome being apprehensive
Get out of your comfort zone and try being on the offensive
Go with your gut because it will help you find food for your soul
Otherwise you'll be miserable and that's definitely not a main
goal

There is nothing for you to lose, only the opportunity
The clock is ticking and you don't apply to perpetuity
If everything fails then at least you gave it a try
Just be happy as much as possible before the day you die

Letting Go

I didn't want to do this but you left me no choice
I guess committing hideous acts is how you rejoice
I have to leave you alone so that means you get disowned
Behavior that causes me to groan will never be condoned

You believed you could do whatever you wanted and always get excused
That is where you messed up, now you're stuck in a daze and confused
No more pardons, apologies or showing you mercy
You're not worthy of a greeting, not even a curtsy

The past doesn't matter because that was then and this is now
You don't even think you're guilty which makes me raise an eyebrow
It boils down to drastic things since I can't get respect from you
Just know that without you I would never have this point of view

You have closed my eyes and also silenced my ears
I can't listen or look at you but I can shed some tears
I'm not heartless at all, I only treat people accordingly
You became annoying and then you started boring me

You see, if you create enough tension then there's a breaking point
Some wounds don't heal with ointment or oil like trying to anoint
Sometimes you have to treat things like allergies and avoid exposure
It may be extreme but that's the only way, it seems, to receive closure

Status doesn't matter, if you act like a criminal then you become expendable
Once upon a time I was amenable until you did things that were untenable
This is the end of the road in case you didn't know
You made it very simple when it came to letting go

Chapter 4

You will always get your share of trial and error
You can be defenseless or you can be a preparer
A lot of things are unforeseen but you can still rise to the occasion
The most important thing will be how you react to the situation

People will try to get inside your head and that's a fact
It will all depend on, whether or not, if your mind is in tact
Low blows like nigger, slut and other diabolical names
Things will go up in flames if you start playing their games

Never get down and dirty, there are a variety of things you can
choose
The split second you stoop down to their level is the moment
you lose
Take a second and just imagine where you will be
Making a guilty plea and on your way to cellblock D

Get use to people's hurtful words and learn to be nonchalant
It's more rewarding when you don't give in to what they want
Remember that children call each other names and always act
farcical
Now you know what you're dealing with if that's a part of their
arsenal

Words pack a punch but you can fight back in another way
Silence is golden so tune out everything that they say
It's not easy to ignore like the ugliest sin but in the long run you
will always win
Through thick and thin, from beginning to the end, you should
have thick skin

Moving On

The feeling is unimaginable and I struggle to come to grips
Feels like my world is destroyed and this is the apocalypse
I've fought before but the biggest fight of my life is trying to
handle your death
I bellow in distress because the pain runs so deep you can't
imagine the depth

The toughest person alive would even drop to their knees
You get to rest in peace but my mind doesn't rest at ease
I'm supposed to be strong but life doesn't prepare you for this
Going through an abyss and the only thing I can do is reminisce

There are so many nights where I just cry myself to sleep
Struggling to hold onto my faith like I'm about to take a leap
Every day is hell and heaven for me because reminders are
everywhere
Too many trips down memory lane and then I realize you're not
there

I tell myself that I'm okay but I'm still under construction
Still teary eyed sometimes when you're part of a discussion
You weren't perfect in the least but some hurt that you caused
hasn't been released
Sometimes I love you and I hate you but I have to let it go
because you are deceased

I wish it was just a sick joke or a really bad dream
I don't have enough self-esteem to face the extreme
I'm completely defenseless against this unthinkable phenomenon
I'm learning to live without you though, just slowly moving on

Compromise

A relationship is a two way street despite what you think
You have to be in sync or the love boat will inevitably sink
You should try something different that you're not use to doing
A new method of operations may cause things to start improving

You don't get to be lazy just because you finally have them
There are plenty of fish in the sea and more than one gem
Don't allow yourself to become complacent
That path could lead to your replacement

It will go a long way if you go out of your way
Do everything in twos just like a cabriolet
Sacrificing for one another might keep things from becoming
monotonous
Otherwise you could see ominous signs that will lead to a bad
consequence

Being selfish all the time doesn't work and it's not very nifty
Give one hundred and ten percent since divorce is fifty-fifty
If you're in love then you'll do most things for your other half
Things like making a warm bubble bath and making them laugh

You never know, you might actually enjoy the feeling
It's better than arguing and letting tempers hit the ceiling
Work for your relationship and it will work out like exercise
Be open to new things and always be willing to compromise

Why I Cheated

I cheated on you and that broke our sacred bond
You believed I was faithful but you were conned
It was an awful thing and I am sincerely sorry that you found out
I can explain but that's probably something you don't want to
hear about

I love the opposite sex and, unfortunately, that's my kryptonite
I never thought this would blow up in my face like dynamite
You had my heart but not my full and undivided attention
I'm too hopeless and there's no hope for my redemption

I just love the attention from all types of random women
Overloaded with excitement from all of the adrenaline
I can't be with one person because it's just not for me
Now I've created bad blood between us like Hepatitis B

This was my secret life and I know it's outrageous
I didn't feel guilty at all because I'm shameless
The women meant nothing to me and I forgot about them in
minutes
But I couldn't get enough and every time I was pushing the limits

I can't fix what I am and my only excuse is that I am a man
I really wanted us to be together forever like a retirement plan
You were severely mistreated, now the love and trust is depleted
It wasn't right at all but this is the only way I can explain why I
cheated

Everybody Lies

You can't hate a liar because you've lied at one time or another
It could've been to protect a friend, yourself, sister or a brother
That's understandable since it is a defense mechanism
But it's viewed as a serious offense like terrorism

It never pays to tell a lie but we do it anyway
Most lies will be transparent just like an x-ray
It's important, saves lives and that's no exaggeration
Imagine telling on someone you love for their incarceration

We tell black lies for our own interests and for something to gain
A red or bloody lie is the worse, only for payback and inflicting
pain
We tell white lies all the time so we can help ourselves and help
out others
Gray lies as well but that doesn't mean lying is pretty because
of all the colors

A lie is still a lie so you can forget about the color code
But never forget the lie you told or the truth will explode
Lies affect the mind over time and can become the truth if you
tell them long enough
The only thing worse than that is a pathological liar who doesn't
know how to bluff

I guess lying is necessary to live your life and I can understand why
It's not even shocking that the word live has to live with a little lie
We all have our reasons for telling a tale so don't let it come as
a surprise
Some people will tell the truth most of the time but everybody
lies

 That's Funny

When certain things happen I can't help but find it comical
It hurts a bit but nothing that requires aid from the hospital
When things hit the fan and I couldn't find a helping hand
I had to laugh because it's better than singing The Blues Band

My so called friends would throw me under the bus
I was in disgust but I had to chuckle rather than fuss
Love interests only liked me after I stopped giving them recognition
Ironic, they thought I would always be around but I'm a limited edition

I signed a contract thinking money is everything and I'll be unhappy if I'm broke
Money can't buy happiness so in the end that turned out to be a hilarious joke
I believed the adults I idolized as a child had great habits to take after
Then I saw their childish ways which provided a whole lot of laughter

I gave homeless people cash and also gave them benefit of the doubt
It was very humorous to found out some of their lives weren't in a drought
I grew up with people who swore that their children would be better than me
It's amusing how some of them never finished high school not even a G.E.D

I always wondered why people mistreated me and I was often riddled
I never understood and over time I just thought about it then giggled
Everything happens for a reason and it won't always be as sweet as honey
But sometimes it plays out in a way that you didn't expect and that's funny

My Mother

My love for her is boundless and I can illustrate it with stories
How she helps me with life, love, school and other categories
She's my guardian angel even though I can't see her halo
That's why I do whatever she wants whenever she says so

She's as fierce and as beautiful as tigers
Keeps me warm like small campfires
I've seen her face things that are unbearable but she persevered
She taught me to do the same and because of that she's so revered

I owe her everything for as long as she lives
She's always selfless with anything that she gives
She would always be direct and made sure I came correct
I think mother means master of the house expects respect

She deserves a red carpet roll-out and handbags for every day of the year
If I could I would buy her diamonds for every finger and for each ear
She knows me so well and maybe because she made me who I am
Always seemed to be a few steps ahead of me and knew every scam

I give her the glory for a childhood that was beyond pleasant
Every Thanksgiving, New Years, Birthday and Christmas present
I know she loves me to death because she's shown me unlike any other
And always wants to keep me close, you can't spell smother without mother

Chapter 5

Not Being Understood

The lights are on but sometimes no one is at home
I will never be alone as long as I have this syndrome
Always worrying and never calm like I'm running from maniacs
I feel like I'm going crazy and helpless against my anxiety attacks

Nervousness is a constant feeling and sometimes I shake
I try working out or just keeping busy for my own sake
I'm not mentally ill and I know that it's all in my head
This isn't depression either because I don't feel like I'm dead

Some might say I'm a pessimist but I'm only battling fear
I dwell on the majority of things that I hear, year after year
There are so many triggers and no hope for a cure
I ask a thousand questions because I'm usually unsure

Most people can't listen because it's just something that they can't comprehend
Since I can't share this with anyone I just wear a mask so I can hide and pretend
I envy others who have better control of their emotions
But I do the best I can just going through the motions

I get so irritated with everyone and I'm not even happy around my loved ones
I often contemplate suicide but I could never use pills, knives or handguns
This isn't my fault but it's certainly problems from my childhood
I've explained this so many times but I'm just not being understood

Something The Eyes Can't See

Looks are nice and all but they can be very deceiving
If you settle for appearance you might be underachieving
The exterior of a car will always grab your attention
But you have to look underneath and examine the engine

That pretty face might not have such a pretty personality
Without any commonality things are destined for mortality
Facial features fade away but that isn't the case with the demeanor
Marry the grim reaper and be as happy as a skyscraper window
cleaner

The eyes can recognize beauty but not a sense of humor
A retina can't tell if a person will be healthy or a tumor
You see a nice body but you don't know if they have a cruel
intention
You can get stuck with a ball and chain with no possible
intervention

If you want to be happy it will take a lot more than just pleasing
the eyes
Focusing on the superficial will cause you to miss something in
disguise
Everyone wants a pretty angel but be on the lookout for Lucifer
Don't dance with anybody because they might be an executioner

You might be in love or you might be confusing it with lust
You could be blinded or seeing a blur from a bit of stardust
People hide things in plain sight so don't let it cost you the
ultimate fee
Be alert because the important things are something the eyes
can't see

Social Media Impact

Communication is the key and it's great to easily access information
However, the reliance and excess use has greatly altered civilization
Always in front of a screen, keypad or keyboard with way too many keystrokes
Think about the time you've spent on apps and websites talking to the same folks

Facebook is great for connecting and keeping in touch
But if you can't talk in person then it has become a crutch
YouTube is entertaining along with being a great source to learn a new skill
You're basically watching television though, so it's another way to stand still

Instagram is nice for sharing pictures and using effects with photography
Then it became a very personal but public photo album along with pornography
Connected to the virtual world but disconnected from the world outside
There is something wrong with that relationship like Bonnie and Clyde

Social media is causing you to become anti-social with people on the street
You can't communicate when you're passing by but you can send a tweet
It's as if you lost your humanity and turned into a robot
Your only concern is if the internet is working and whatnot

Linked into way too many things like snapchat, yahoo, msn and
Google
All these distractions are like being asleep with no one to play
the bugle
It's benefited the world but it hurt the way people interact
You were severely affected by the social media impact

Too Proud

Pleasant, risky, individual, deadly, and earnest
Having too much is like being sick without an internist
Don't swallow your pride; just get rid of it instead
Never ingest it because you might cause it to spread

Too proud to do a lot of things and I know how you feel
Pride is good but not when it's as big as a Ferris wheel
If you can't admit when you're wrong then you can thank your
pride
Whatever or whoever told you that was acceptable definitely lied

You can be too proud to allow yourself to hit rock bottom
But if you're too proud to ask for help then that's a problem
You're only making it worse if you can't say you're sorry
If you keep this up then your future will turn out gnarly

Tread lightly with pride because it can lead to your demise
It could also lead to humbleness and the ability to empathize
Having too much pride is a lot like having a huge ego
You can be proud but don't think you're a lion like a Leo

Don't forget pride isn't all about self, it can be anew
For example, you could make others proud of you
Be better and wiser by setting yourself away from the crowd
Don't let things slip out of your life by being too proud

A Positive Person

No matter what there is always beauty in every opportunity
It doesn't have to be terror in every error so use your ingenuity
Being negative has never helped in any situation
It will only bring the status quo to degradation

Things will always get harder before they get better
You can bet on that so you'll never feel like a debtor
Pessimism is the enemy so put a little optimism into your system
A negative mind is ill but positivity can get rid of that symptom

An optimist will see the good and will look for a solution
A pessimist has negative questions and no good contribution
Positive people go far in life and have a more attractive personality
The kind of people that you want in your corner and their mentality

If you can't be positive then don't say a word
Negativity is contagious and can be transferred
It's simply a state of mind so try to get your mind right
It's easy to be negative but resist with all of your might

Just be happy go lucky and be a realist as well
Weight will be lifted like releasing a barbell
Mishaps will occur and when things start to worsen
The best thing you can do is be a positive person

Technological Takeover

Welcome to the twenty-first century where everyone owns an electronic device
Laptops, cellphones and desktop computers just to be precise
They're all useful tools but they've now become limbs
They're valued so much like they're these precious gems

A new cellphone gets released and the price is sky high
We just want to interact through a touch screen and Wi-Fi
Spending so much time on an android that we might become an android
Mobile phones and chargers along with the internet keep us overjoyed

Rest in peace to a time where everything wasn't recorded and uploaded
Young children didn't have iPads and playgrounds weren't eroded
You could call anyone and not talk to a machine that's voice automated
Everyone spent most of their time outside and not indoors being isolated

Technology is worthwhile and nations need it worldwide
But it has been taken for granted and used for genocide
We put more faith into technology than we put into mankind
We can't compete in the workplace so we're fired or reassigned

We're not really blinded we're just merely distracted
Maybe technology should be a little subtracted
It shouldn't be this way but technology made a breakthrough
A technological takeover and there's nothing that we can do

I'm not entirely sure if I'm a free person or if I'm programmed
So many things put into my brain that is continuously jammed
The world insists that you live by a lot of unspoken rules
The masses are taught and guided like a bunch of mules

Apparently I'm a loser if I'm not married by the age of thirty
Don't drink alcohol too early, drink something else if you're thirsty
School or being a bum are your only two options
I guess work was never a part of the adoptions

A man isn't a real man unless he owns a car and knows how to
change a tire
A woman should know how to cook, clean and operate a washer
and dryer
Men should have strong backs, lots of muscles, jobs and nice
haircuts
Women should have small waists, large breasts, big lips and
round butts

Being a male virgin isn't cool so lose your virginity as fast as
you can
Women have to save theirs until marriage or they won't be
desired by any man
Keep up with the latest fads just so you don't become an outcast
Eventually settle down, have children and then retire at long last

Tattoos along with piercings are unacceptable and don't belong
on your skin
No friends of the opposite sex if you're in a relationship unless
they're your kin
Everything would be fine if there was a little more variety
You can't live privately because of the psychology of society

Chapter 6

The N Word

It started off as a small word that was slowly amplified
Freely used but then only certain colors were qualified
Now it's a sensitive word that was forced to be abbreviated
People are intimidated to say it out of fear of being assassinated

It's believed that there's a difference between the words nigga
and nigger
Just like there's a difference between an opportunist and a gold
digger
The color of your skin shouldn't matter since it will always be a
racial slur
Dark-skinned individuals are demeaning themselves whether or
not if they concur

Anyone that's light skinned says it and it's a serious offense
Even if it was in a friendly way you still can't recompense
Punishing people for using it today is absolutely absurd
They had nothing to do with the history and it's only a word

Throughout the years this magical word has changed its definition
It was ignorance and now it's an offensive term according to the
exposition
It's constantly used and everyone knows that it's wrong
But it's glamorized by music artists when they say it in a song

No one will be offended if it's taken out of the conversation
Only then will it be buried and cut off from wide circulation
Until then it will grab attention and won't keep people calm
The N word went nuclear and is now stronger than an F bomb

Ridiculousness In Racism

Hatred towards a group of people and never given a good reason
That sounds just as bizarre as someone committing an act of treason
Something stupid and utterly outrageous that you were taught
No one can blame you but if you hold onto that then it's your fault

It's completely okay to hate people for their ethnic backgrounds
You can just say that out loud and listen to how crazy it sounds
You never know what could happen so you should get rid of the hate
Fate might have that race be the only one that your child will date

One day an angel might help you out and you'll be the sadist
That person might be black or white and you'll be a racist
It could also play out differently and not have such a happy ending
You might hate them so much you'd rather suffer than try befriending

Whatever you believe about a group of people is just a disgrace
The way people act and behave isn't bias towards race
Don't be so naïve and believe in a rumor or a stereotype
You'll see in time like waiting for a fruit to get ripe

Stop and think for yourself because some things should be questioned
One way of thinking doesn't have to be permanent, it can be freshened
Don't live inside a box or a rectangular prism
Open your eyes to the ridiculousness in racism

The Power Of Money

Currency is worth a lot more than you think
It comes and it goes faster than you can blink
You can never have enough so you keep stuffing your pockets
Might give an arm or a leg and rip them right from their sockets

Cash distracts you so the important things aren't always clear
You've believed that money means, my only need every year
You might sell your soul for whatever its worth
In exchange for riches to get heaven on earth

Travel a great distance by taking long drives or going on long walks
Doing whatever it says whenever the money talks
You will almost never see money in the lost and found
No surprise there since it makes the world go round

It might be false or money might be the root of all evil
But it doesn't force you to do things that are illegal
Don't let money manipulate you just so you can maintain a certain status
Problems will follow and make you feel like you're handling a cactus

Money is very important and that's why you go to work
But living to only get paid is how you slowly go berserk
Now you can see how it influences you and it might be a bit funny
It's supposed to work like that though, that's the power of money

Traveling Is Good Treatment

Having the same routine day after day might drive you a little
insane
You see the same nouns when you ride the bus, drive or take
the train
Everything might make you sick and now it's time for a strong
medicine
Well a little getaway could make you feel better than you've ever
been

Try broadening your horizons by seeing some new horizons
It's full of excitement like a high speed chase with police sirens
There are many things to do when you're not feeling good
Like escaping the simple boundaries of your neighborhood

Start saving a little change to make a change in the scenery
Don't exist just to work because people aren't machinery
See something different and it doesn't have to be a great distance
It can easily happen but that will depend on your persistence

Everyone in the world has something that they've always wanted
to see
Perhaps Africa or the home of Jack Daniels in Lynchburg,
Tennessee
Maybe even Pisa, Italy to see the famous leaning tower of Pisa
If you're an art lover then go to Paris, France to see the Mona Lisa

You'll enjoy it because it's relaxing and therapeutic
Just like the feeling when you listen to good music
Go and make the trip whenever your time is convenient
And you can rest assured that traveling is good treatment

Living Inside A Box

It's so depressing when there is no room to grow
Kind of like cars with flat tires and nowhere to go
Locked inside a cell and they're the ones who locked it
Comfortable as can be like wearing a favorite outfit

There's no innovation or motivation so they just follow the herd
The sky could be the limit but they don't want to imitate a bird
It's okay, I suppose, to live your life in a small pond
I just thought everyone would like to go above and beyond

Unaware and don't care about the world outside
As long as they're sheltered then they're satisfied
No such thing as free will or experiencing a new thrill
And moving forward for them is like running on a treadmill

Completely settled and content with life's regular procedures
They keep the same company because new people are creatures
Never bored living a life surrounded by cardboard
The only thing that's missing is not having a landlord

It's hard to fathom that being so enclosed doesn't make them
feel claustrophobic
Maybe they're just as tough as nails and have mastered the art
of being a stoic
A world that's full of self-made boundaries and roadblocks
They're at their home sweet home and living inside a box

Hard To Be Beautiful

She uses all of these cosmetics so she can be a ten out of ten
It's hard work and requires a lot of time like big ben
It's not enough to just have natural beauty
Getting dolled up has now become a duty

She's a little self-conscious because she compares herself to other women
She doesn't want to be an ugly duckling so becoming a swan is the mission
Always critiquing her body and making sure everything looks great
She might be happy with some things but never ask about her weight

She wants to be elegant for herself so her image has to be perfected
Sometimes she does it for someone else and she probably gets neglected
So much energy is spent on herself that she should definitely feel confident
At this point she's entitled to some attention and even a compliment

She has to do a lot more than a man when it comes to getting ready
Moisturizer, concealer and foundation requires hands that are steady
There are so many eyes involved and it all starts with a primer
Eyelids, eyebrows and eye shadow but if not then just eyeliner

That's only her face so imagine that in addition to doing her hair
Then she does all of her nails and that's an entirely different affair
She will do whatever it takes but it has to be suitable
She has made it very clear that it's hard to be beautiful

Chapter 7

Being Overprotective

My parents are so irritating and always on me like cologne or perfume
I wish I had privacy but it's nonexistent nor do I have any elbow room
I could swear that I have two personal bodyguards
There's more spotlight on me than prison courtyards

They're so fearful that something bad will happen to me
God forbid I get sick, cut or a scrape on the knee
They should know that the world is designed for me to get hurt
Pain is coming no matter what like something you can't divert

I'm to the point where I keep secrets and strictly tell lies
I know it's something that they despise but they act like spies
When I become an adult I will definitely be moving far away
I'll visit on certain holidays and when it's someone's birthday

What started off as a concern has now turned into an obsession
I know it's out of love but I'm tired of living under repression
They're only hurting me by trying to be my private facilitator
They won't always be around when serious matters come later

I can explain it a thousand ways but they don't listen to a child
A little freedom to them is like allowing me to run wild
I feel like I'm a fugitive and can't outrun the detective
They really get on my last nerve being overprotective

We Don't Want A War

We can't come together in peace so it leads to bloodshed
Things will be fine after people are bright and brick red
Most people don't fully understand exactly what that means
Murder in reality is more vivid than high definition screens

The youth fight for their country and will be in front of the warpath
That's only the beginning and no one can prepare for the aftermath
Family and friends will have to say a very early goodbye
Because a majority of these men and women will ultimately die

Survivors of the war return to their lives but appear to be a little out of order
Some are amputees and a lot of them have a post-traumatic stress disorder
A combat veteran usually fights a lot of bad memories and nightmares
A thankless job and it's hard to find someone who genuinely cares

War hurts a country's population but also hurts it economically
People who want to kill to gain something aren't thinking logically
War involves hidden agendas that come at a great expense
It will always make cents but it never makes any sense

Mankind should be focusing on taking civilization to greater heights
Not focusing on killing each other and then building memorial sites
It only ends in tears with heartache and gore
Believe me when I say we don't want a war

Alcohol Intake

The only beverage that requires you to drink responsibly
And then there are other things that you hear constantly
Alcohol is the devil and never make it a part of your diet
If you do then you'll behave irrational and cause a riot

It's always the majority that ruins it for the minority
Bad news is always first because it has superiority
Everything that's said isn't always true so it might be a myth
Individuals try to get many things set in stone like a monolith

Alcohol affects everyone differently but still takes heed
The effects can creep up on you fast with sonic speed
Shots of alcohol back to back will make a good time come to an
early end
Height and weight are a factor and remember water is your best
friend

Drinking to get inebriated on a regular basis is just insane
Enjoyment can be one beer or one glass of champagne
Most people don't know their limit nor do they watch their drink
They like to skate on thin ice over a frozen lake instead of a rink

Alcohol has an infamous reputation and it can be cancerous
It's still glamorous and occasionally causes souls to feel amorous
People drink recklessly and pay for it the next day when they're
awake
Alcohol just has to be balanced but people can't handle their
alcohol intake

 Karma

She might be an unfriendly female canine but you gave her a
motive
And there's nothing you can do to get away from this explosive
What she has planned for you will make her seem villainous
Her naughty list is endless compared to the one of Saint Nicholas

She's the hardest and most effective teacher but can't be found
in a school
It doesn't matter where you go because your debts will soon be
paid in full
She's the deliverer of what goes around and comes around
Also the one driving the bus when people pin you to the ground

You'll never see her coming so you might as well be wearing a
blindfold
Her revenge will be a dish that can be served piping hot or ice
cold
You could be served as the main course or as a hors d'oeuvre
The bottom line is you'll ultimately get what you deserve

She can't be persuaded; she only acts and never makes a threat
Don't think she'll overlook you because you aren't dead yet
Equal opportunity has always been there she put your fate in
your hands
You're the reason why your world unraveled down to the last
strands

She isn't shy at all so you could say she's an extrovert
But she could still torture you and then watch you hurt
She surrounds you entirely and becomes a part of your aura
She'll make you a believer if you don't believe in karma

A Broken Home

Two adults can no longer live together so one of them has to split
Now the child has to go with the parent who is most fit
This will play a key role in their development as they begin their stride
Putting a child on a roller-coaster and they're not old enough for the ride

The adults' offspring has already loss some of their stability
And probably in the middle, occasionally, of their parents' hostility
It's more than likely that one parent is a bit jealous and immature
That just adds onto the work load that a child shouldn't endure

The relationship between them and one of their parents could be lopsided
They're put in a position where their love, in a way, has to be divided
If their parents live close then they won't have to switch schools for education
Otherwise they'll travel back and forth every holiday and summer vacation

If everything turns out alright then this won't be passed down so it can repeat
Parents should want a better life for their child with whomever they meet
Unless they want their grandchildren to also be stuck in a quandary
A family should either clean up or get rid of their dirty laundry

It would have been a lot better if things were just repaired
No one is spared from this tragedy and they're always unprepared
This is what happens when a family separates then packs and moves like Styrofoam
If the mother and father don't work things out then they'll be left with a broken home

Alone In Death

Dying is the last part of your life so you know it's inevitable
You can be cremated or buried with a gravestone that's legible
You go empty-handed so everything gets left behind
The lives intertwined with yours will soon unwind

You can't take anyone with you but there's an upside
You can have someone next to you by your bedside
Don't let it upset you too much and get under your skin
You shouldn't believe that you'll never see them again

Your book closes but you move onto the next chapter
Remaining here in memory while you're in the hereafter
Death might not be as bad as most people make it out to be
Life is difficult so in death you're more than likely carefree

The body is temporary so you're inhabiting a shell
Your true self isn't visible to you like a parallel
The soul lasts forever so forget about your flesh
You have to move on so you can start afresh

Till death do us part doesn't apply only to marriage
You can't leave the way you came in like a miscarriage
Everyone gets separated like a paper wastebasket
You're alone in death it's only one per casket

Love For Music

If silence is golden then music must be platinum
Favorite songs must be turned up to the maximum
Be thankful for ears and most importantly the discovery of sound
Whoever that person was they should have definitely been crowned

Music is a healthy addiction regardless of the genre
Try living without it and you'll have all kinds of trauma
Think of a few rough times and then you'll probably see
Music was playing to help you get to where you needed to be

It can give you goosebumps and sometimes even touch your soul
Whether or not it's jazz, rap, house, techno, blues or rock and roll
Music gathers people around and it's all love not hate
Music means mainly used so individuals cooperate

It never fades away and it will never lose its appeal
Always stays alive whether its mp3 or reel-to-reel
It doesn't ask for much except for a dance or a standing ovation
It causes a little perspiration but you'll be happy after the duration

It sets the ambience anywhere and can be tantalizing
Giving life to a party because it's so energizing
It plays with our emotions which can be a good or bad influence
But have love for music and the musicians with their instruments